D0056618

BELLY LAUGH
RIDDLES
AND PUNS
for Kids

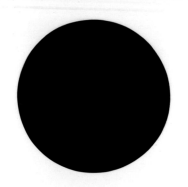

BELLY LAUGH RIDDLES AND PUNS for Kids

350 Hilarious Riddles and Puns

Sky Pony
New York

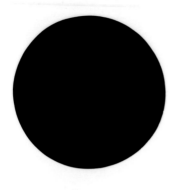

Special thanks to:
Bethany Straker for her fabulous
illustrations

Sky Pony Press books may be purchased in bulk at special discounts for
sales promotion, corporate gifts, fund-raising, or educational purposes.
Special editions can also be created to specifications. For details, contact
the Special Sales Department, Sky Pony Press, 307 West 36th Street, 11th
Floor, New York, NY 10018 or info@skyhorsepublishing.com.

Sky Pony® is a registered trademark of Skyhorse Publishing, Inc.®, a
Delaware corporation.

Visit our website at www.skyponypress.com.

10 9 8 7 6 5 4 3

Manufactured in China, July 2016
This product conforms to CPSIA 2008

Library of Congress Cataloging-in-Publication Data

Cover design by Gretchen Schuler

Print ISBN: 978-1-5107-1198-3
Ebook ISBN:978-1-5107-1199-0

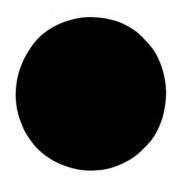

BELLY LAUGH
RIDDLES AND PUNS
for Kids

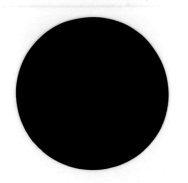

Q: Which month has 28 days?

A: They all do!

Q: What word is always spelled wrong?

A: Wrong.

Q: What has two hands but can't clap?

A: A clock.

Q: What gets damper as it dries?

   A: A towel.

The best way to communicate with fish is to drop them a line.

Q: What has four legs, one head, and only one foot?

A: A bed.

Q: Can a frog jump higher than the Empire State Building?

A: Of course, the Empire State Building can't jump.

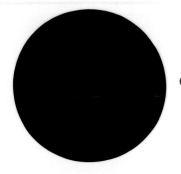

Q: **Who always sleeps with their shoes on?**

A: Horses

Q: **What can you never eat for breakfast?**

A: Lunch and dinner

Q: **What can you maintain without saying anything?**

A: Silence.

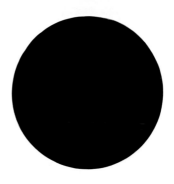

Q: **What is really easy to get into but difficult to get out of?**

A: Trouble

A dad bought a donkey for his son because he thought he might get a kick out of it.

Q: **What is difficult to keep, hold, or destroy?**

A: A secret

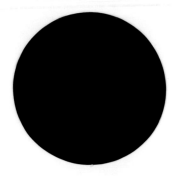

Q: **What fills up a room but takes up no space?**

A: Darkness.

Q: **What has two words, starts with P, ends with E, and has thousands of letters?**

A: Post Office

Q: **What animal asks too many questions?**

A: An owl

The best way to stop a charging bull is to take away his credit card.

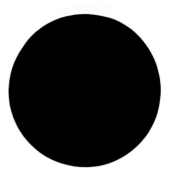

Q: What is something you can catch but you can't throw it?

A: A cold.

A chicken crossing the road is poultry in motion.

Q: What type of room has no doors?

A: A mushroom.

Q: When is homework no longer homework?

A: When you turn it in to the teacher.

Q: Railroad. How do you spell that without any R's?

A: T-H-A-T

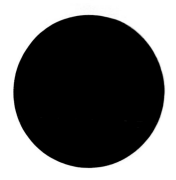

Q: What's black and white and red all over?

A: An embarrassed zebra.

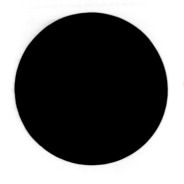

Q: What can travel around the world but stays in the corner?

A: A stamp.

Q: What is larger than you but weighs nothing?

A: Your shadow.

Q: Why are calendars so busy?

A: They have a lot of dates.

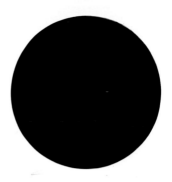

I couldn't figure out how lightning worked and then it struck me.

He's been to the dentist on many occasions so he knew the drill.

Q: What goes up but never comes back down?

A: Your age.

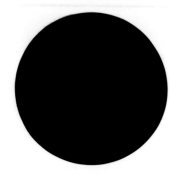

Q: **What is the slipperiest country?**

A: Greece!

Q: **What occurs twice in one moment, once in a millennium, but never in a hundred years?**

A: The letter M.

It was an emotional wedding. Even the cake was in tiers.

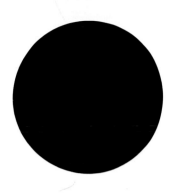

Q: **What has a head and a tail but no legs?**

A: A penny.

Chalkboards are remarkable.

Q: **Which side of the dog has the most hair?**

A: The outside.

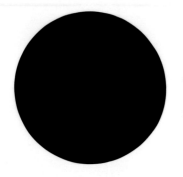

Time flies like an arrow but fruit flies like a banana.

Q: What do you find at the end of a rainbow?

A: W!

Q: What's a snake's favorite subject in school?

A: Hissstory.

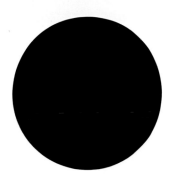

Q: What touches every continent but has no beginning, middle, or end?

A: The Ocean.

Q: What never asks a question but needs an answer?

A: A telephone.

Q: Why are brooms always late?

A: They usually oversweep.

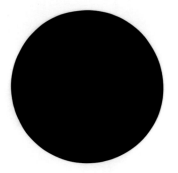

Q: **What do ghosts wear on**

  their feet?

A: BOO-ts.

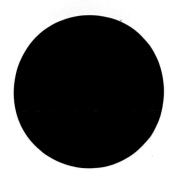

Q: **What can go up and down without moving?**

A: Stairs.

Q: **What must you break before you can use it?**

A: An egg.

Q: **What do you throw away when you want to use it?**

A: An anchor.

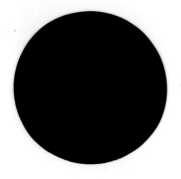

Q: What is full of keys but

can't open any doors?

A: A piano.

Exit signs. They're on the way out.

Q: What has no life but can still die?

A: A battery.

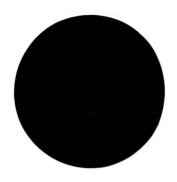

Q: What will die if you give it water?

A: Fire.

Q: How many apples can you fit in an empty box?

A: None! If you put apples in it, the box won't be empty anymore.

Q: What word is shorter when you add two letters to it?

A: Short.

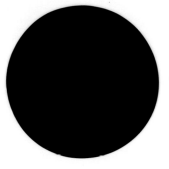

Q: What is as big as a dinosaur but weighs less than a dinosaur?

A: A dinosaur's shadow.

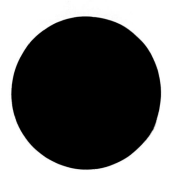

Q: What is yours but gets used by others more?

A: Your name.

Q: What shows up at night and disappears in the day time but you can always find in Hollywood?

A: Stars.

Q: What's one way to double your money?

A: Put it front of a mirror.

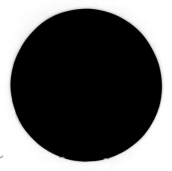

Q: What do you hold without touching it?

A: A conversation.

Q: What insect can you spell with one letter?

A: Bee.

Q: What is the capital of Hawaii?

A: H.

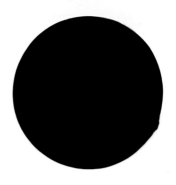

Q: When is the moon the heaviest?

A: When it's full.

Q: What can run but can't walk?

A: A river.

Q: What do people and animals make but you can't see?

A: Noise.

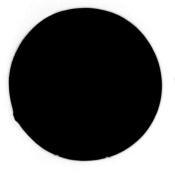

Q: What has a back and four
   legs but no body?

A: A chair.

He tried to catch fog but mist.

Q: What kind of coach has no wheels?

A: A baseball coach.

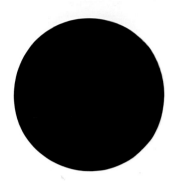

Q: **What kind of tree do you find in the kitchen?**

A: A pantry.

Q: **What ten-letter word starts with g-a-s?**

A: Automobile.

Q: **What time is the same spelled both forward and backwards?**

A: Noon.

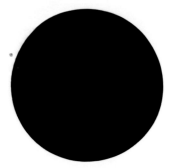

Q: Where will you always find money?

A: In the dictionary.

Q: If money grew on trees, what would everyone's favorite season be?

A: Fall.

Q: Why is Rudolph the Red Nosed Reindeer so good at trivia?

A: He NOSE a lot.

Once you've seen one shopping center, you've seen a mall.

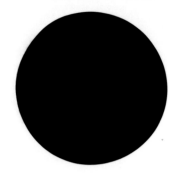

Q: Why did the farmer plant a light bulb?

A: He wanted to grow a power plant.

Long stories about knights tend to dragon.

Q: How did Benjamin Franklin feel after he discovered electricity?

A: He was shocked.

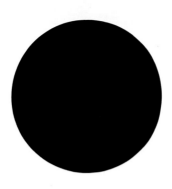

Q: What does a nuclear scientist do in her spare time?

A: Goes fission.

Q: What is burned by cars that are driven at night?

A: The midnight oil.

Q: When you're looking for a lost remote, why is it always in the last place you looked?

A: Because once you find it, you stop looking.

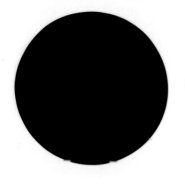

Q: **What thrives in winter,**
   dies in summer, and its
   roots grow upward?

A: An icicle.

Q: **How can a person go 7 days without sleep?**

A: He or she only sleeps at night.

Q: **What has four fingers and one thumb but is not**
   alive?

A: A glove.

Q: **What is as light as air but something that even the strongest person can't hold for more than five minutes?**

A: Breath.

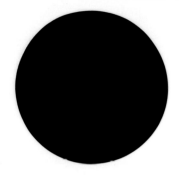

Q: **Name three consecutive days without saying Wednesday, Friday, or Sunday.**

Λ: Yesterday, today, and tomorrow.

Q: **What has three feet but cannot walk, dance, or run?**

A: A yardstick.

Q: **A man is running a marathon and passes the person in second place, what place is he now in?**

A: Second place.

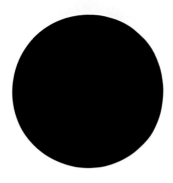

Q: Which vegetable can your father make with Scissors?

A: Pa snips.

Q: What is full of holes but still holds water?

A: A sponge.

Q: If dogs have fleas, what do sheep have?

A: Fleece.

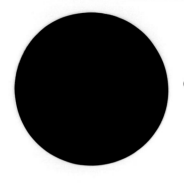

Q: **What starts out tall but gets shorter the longer it stands?**

A: A candle.

Q: **What side of the rabbit has the most fur?**

A: The outside.

Q: **What is broken with only one word?**

A: Silence.

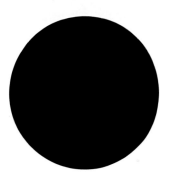

Life lesson: Never trust atoms.

They make everything up.

Q: What has six legs but only walks around on four?

A: A rider on her horse.

Q: What is always on its way but never arrives?

A: Tomorrow.

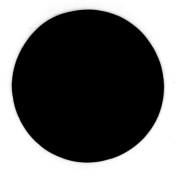

Q: **What has no beginning**
or end and nothing in the
middle?

A: A doughnut.

Q: **Do you know how expensive mixed nuts are?**

A: Very. It costs an almond a leg.

He used to have a fear of hurdles until one day he
got over it.

Q: What is red when it's in
      use, black when it's not,
      and gray when you throw
      it out?

A: Coal.

Being struck by lightning is a shocking experience.

Q: What do you bring out on the table to cut but
    never eat?

A: A deck of cards.

Q: Why do you never see dragons out during the day?

A: Because they like to hunt knights.

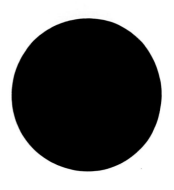

Q: **What do you think is**

the most popular use of

cowhide?

A: To cover cows, of course.

Q: **What does a dog have that no other animal**

has?

A: Puppies!

Q: **When is it possible for Friday to come before**

Thursday?

A: In the dictionary.

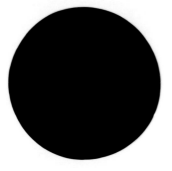

There was once a blanket factory in town, but the company folded.

Q: What building has the most stories?

A: A library.

Q: What can you sit on, sleep on, and brush your teeth with?

A: A chair, a bed, and a toothbrush.

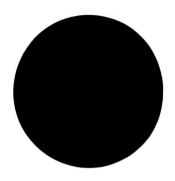

Q: Where's the best place to buy pens?

A: Pennsylvania.

Q: Who can shave over twenty times a day and still have a beard?

A: A barber.

Q: Four children and two dogs weren't standing under an umbrella so how did none of them get wet?

A: It wasn't raining.

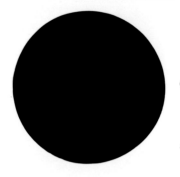

Q: **What can you keep after giving to someone else?**

A: A promise.

Q: **What do you always answer without a question?**

A: A telephone.

A perfectly spherical pumpkin makes good pi.

Q: **What can you put in your pocket that keeps it empty?**

A: A hole.

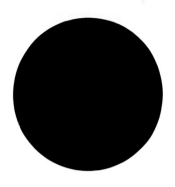

Q: **What is tiny and sharp and has one eye?**

A: A needle.

Q: **What is there a lot of in the Pacific Ocean?**

A: Water.

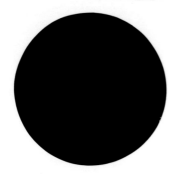

Q: **What looks like half of an apple?**

A: The other half.

Q: **Where do wealthy people eat their poultry?**

A: In the chicken wing.

People who eat candy with two hands are ambi-dextrose.

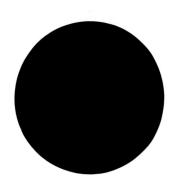

Q: **What is the first thing Elizabeth I did when she came to the throne?**

A: Sit on it.

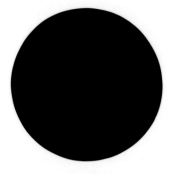

Q: **Why do you have to go to bed?**

A: Because your bed won't come to you!

Q: **What is a disastrous cat called?**

A: A catastrophe.

Q: **Why is it a bad idea to tell a joke while you're playing ice hockey?**

A: Because the ice might crack up.

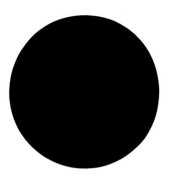

I was going to tell you a funny joke about a boomerang but I forgot. I'm sure it will come back to me.

Q: How did the portrait end up in police custody?

A: It was framed.

Q: What runs and whistles but can't walk or talk?

A: A train.

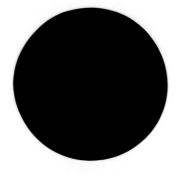

Q: Why can leopards never escape from the zoo?

A: They are always spotted.

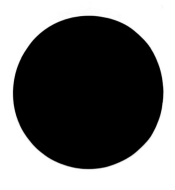

Q: Why are boats and shops alike?

A: One has sails and the other has sales.

Q: What gets older but doesn't age?

A: A portrait

Q: What's hard to maintain but easily broken?

A: Silence.

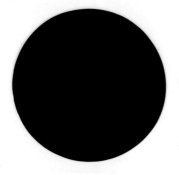

Q: **What do you call a small wound?**

A: A short cut.

I wanted to look for my missing watch but I couldn't find the time.

Q: **Which pet makes the most noise?**

A: A trumpet.

Q: When is a ring square?

A: When it's a boxing ring.

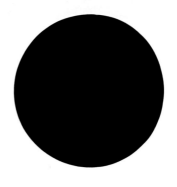

She tried to eat a clock but it was very time consuming.

Q: What would you call a pun sandwich?

A: A Punini

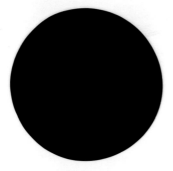

Q: What does a winner lose in a race?

A: His breath.

Q: What's the best way to keep in touch with the ocean life?

A: Drop them a line.

Q: What has thirty heads and thirty tails?

A: Thirty quarters.

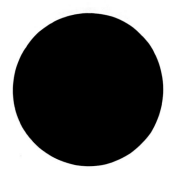

Q: **What can you see better as it gets darker?**

A: Stars.

Q: What starts with T, ends with T, and is full of T?

A: A teapot.

Q: What has wings and can fly but is not a bird or an insect?

A: A plane.

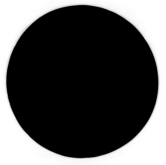

Q: **What can you never hold in your right hand?**

A: Your right hand.

Q: **What kind of coat is always wet when you put it on?**

A: A coat of paint.

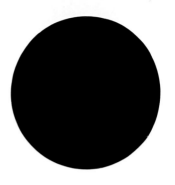

Q: How many seconds are there in one year?

A: 12

- January 2nd
- February 2nd
- March 2nd
- April 2nd
- May 2nd
- June 2nd
- July 2nd
- August 2nd
- September 2nd
- October 2nd
- November 2nd
- December 2nd

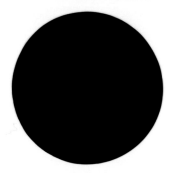

Q: **What do you call a bear**

without an ear?

A: A "b"

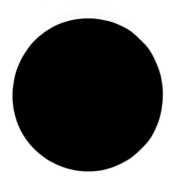

Q: What's the most curious
   letter?

A: Y.

Q: The man who made it doesn't want it. The man
   who bought it doesn't need it. The man who
   needs it doesn't know it. What is it?

A: A coffin.

Q: What does December have that the other
   months don't have?

A: The letter D.

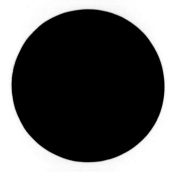

Q: **What does down but never comes up?**

A: Rain

Q: **What type of tree can you carry in your hand?**

A: A palm.

Q: **What can go up a chimney but can't go down a chimney up?**

A: An umbrella.

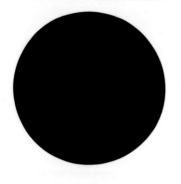

Q: **If you are what you eat, what should you stay away from?**

A: The nuts.

Q: **How do you make the number one vanish?**

A: Add a "G" to it and it's gone!

Q: **What has a neck but not a head?**

A: A bottle.

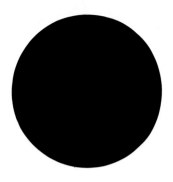

Q: What is something you can hear but not see or touch?

A: Your voice.

Q: What goes uphill and downhill but always stays in the same place?

A: A road.

Q: Why did the man put a clock in a safe?

A: He wanted to save time.

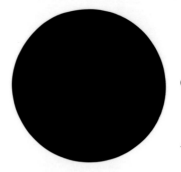

Q: Which letter of the alphabet is not me?

A: U.

Q: How is the letter "A" like noon?

A: It's right in the middle of the day.

Q: Which letter of the alphabet would you say is the fullest of water?

A: The letter "C"

Q: **What's as big as a horse but doesn't weigh anything?**

A: A horse's shadow.

To write with a broken pencil is pointless.

Q: What are the two strongest days of the week?

A: Saturday and Sunday—the rest are weak days.

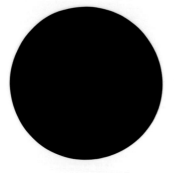

Oranges are very a-peeling.

Q: What's the difference between electricity and lightning?

A: You don't have to pay for lightning.

Q: Why are baseball stadiums so cool?

A: There's a fan in every seat.

People love crazy glue.

They're very attached to it.

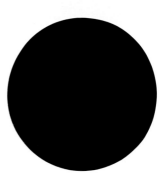

Q: What has waves but isn't the ocean?

A: Hair.

Q: What has teeth but can't bite?

A: A comb.

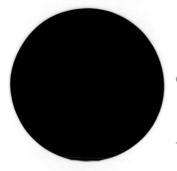

Q: What falls but never breaks?

A: Night.

The old batteries were distributed free of charge.

Q: What breaks but never falls?

A: Day.

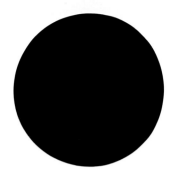

Q: What will break if it falls?

A: Glass.

Q: Which letter of the alphabet stings?

A: B.

Q: What loses its head in the morning and gets it back at night?

A: A pillow.

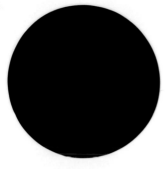

Yesterday a clown held the door open for someone. It was a nice jester.

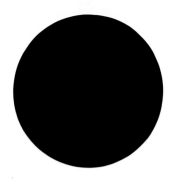

Q: What asks but never answers?

A: An owl.

Q: During what month do people sleep the least?

A: February—it's the shortest.

Q: Who builds bridges of silver and crowns of gold?

A: A dentist.

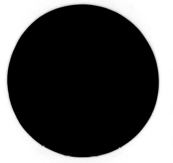

He couldn't quite understand the angle his math teacher was going for.

Q: What has six eyes but can't see anything?

A: The three blind mice.

Q: What do ghosts wear on their feet?

A: BOOts.

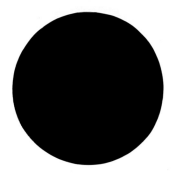

Glass windows are such a pane.

Q: What type of sea creature can help you build a house?

A: A hammerhead shark.

Q: What has forests with no trees, rivers without water, roads without cars, and deserts without sand?

A: A map.

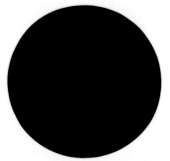

He didn't like his beard at first but then it grew on him.

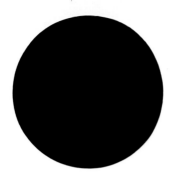

Q: **What can you break easily without ever touching it or seeing it?**

A: A promise.

Q: **Why do sharks only swim in salt water?**

A: Pepper water makes them sneeze.

Q: **What do you call a cat with one leg?**

A: A cat.

Q: The more you take, the
   more you leave behind.
   What is it?

A: Footsteps.

Q: What do you throw away when you want to use
   and take in when you want to use it?

A: An anchor.

Q: What will always come but never arrive today?

A: Tomorrow.

Q: **What goes around all cities and towns but never comes inside?**

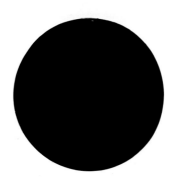

A: Streets.

Q: **What has no life but can die?**

A: A battery.

Q: **What is always answered but never asks a question?**

A: A doorbell.

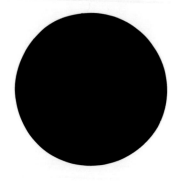

Q: **What has a lot of memories but owns nothing?**

A: A picture frame.

Q: **What goes up when water comes down?**

A: An umbrella.

Q: **What's the day after yesterday?**

A: Today!

Q: What's the worst thing about throwing a party in space?

A: You have to planet!

Jackhammers. They're groundbreaking.

Q: What occurs twice in a week, once in a year, but never in a day?

A: The letter "e"

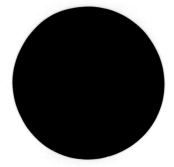

Q: How do you make antifreeze?

A: You take away her sweater!

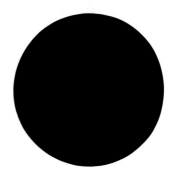

A gossip is someone with a great sense of rumor.

Q: Which word in the dictionary is always spelled incorrectly?

A: Incorrectly.

Q: How do you make fruit punch?

A: Put an apple in a boxing glove.

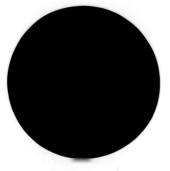

Vinyl records.

They're groovy.

Q: What does a spy do when he gets cold?

A: He goes undercover.

Q: Why are rivers always rich?

A: Because they have two banks.

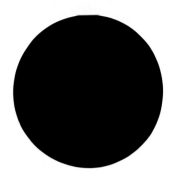

Q: What turns without moving?

A: Milk. It can turn sour.

Q: What part of your body has the most rhythm?

A: Eardrums.

Past, present, and future were hanging out. It was tense.

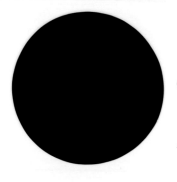

Q: **How is the letter "E" like London?**

A: Because "E" is the capital of England.

Q: **How many apples can you fit in an empty box?**

A: Zero. If you put an apple in it, it won't be empty anymore.

If towels could tell jokes they would probably have a dry sense of humor.

82

Q: Did you hear about the guy who got a brain transplant?

A: He wasn't going to originally get it but changed his mind.

Q: What happened when the comedian tried to tell a chemistry joke?

A: She didn't get a reaction.

Q: What happened to the girl reading the book on anti-gravity?

A: It was impossible to put down.

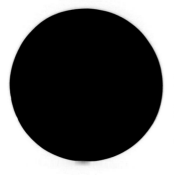

It's hard to explain puns to a kleptomaniac. They always take everything literally.

His fear of heights has elevated his heartrate.

Q: Did you hear about the guy who got fired from the calendar factory?

A: All he did was take a day off.

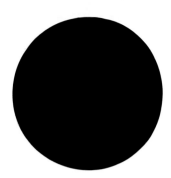

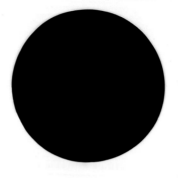

Q: If there are three apples
and you take away two,
how many do you have?

A. Two.

Q: What can fill up a room but take up no space?

A: Light.

Q: What falls but never gets hurt?

A: Snow.

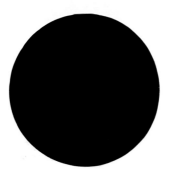

He went to a seafood disco last week and pulled a mussel.

Q: What has a tongue but cannot talk?

A: A shoe.

Q: What has one eye and cannot see?

A: A needle.

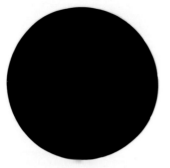

When a clock is hungry it always goes back for seconds.

Q: When is the best time to eat eggs?

A: The crack of dawn.

Q: What kind of shoes do frogs wear?

A: Open-toad.

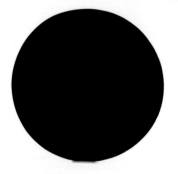

Q: **What is a plumber's favorite shoe?**

A: Clogs.

Q: **What do you call chandeliers?**

A: High lights.

Math teachers who retire call it the "aftermath."

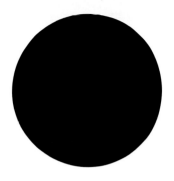

Q: What do you call a fake noodle?

A: An impasta.

The person who invented the door knock must have won the no-bell prize.

Q: How do Vikings communicate?

A: Norse code.

The thief who stole the

calendar got twelve months.

Q: Which day do chickens hate the most?

A: Fry-day

Q: Why did the lobster cross the road?

A: To get to the other tide.

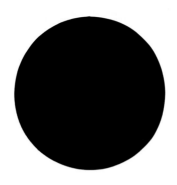

Q: What do you call a dinosaur with a big vocabulary?

A: A thesaurus.

Q: What do you call an alligator in a vest?

A: An investigator.

Q: How far can a fox run into a field?

A: Halfway. And then he's running out of it.

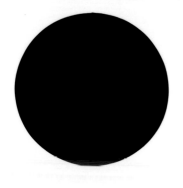

Q: How many bananas can you eat on an empty stomach?

A: Just one. After that it's not empty anymore.

Q: What does an orthodontist do in a fight?

A: He braces himself.

Q: Why did the builder hate glass windows?

A: Glass windows are such a pane.

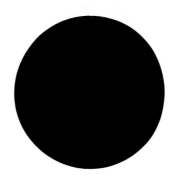

Q: What can you never eat for lunch?

A: Breakfast or dinner!

Q: Where is the ocean the deepest?

A: The bottom.

Q: How is the letter A like a flower?

A: Because the B is always after it.

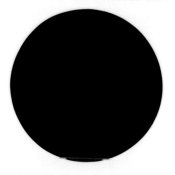

Q: **What do you call a dish masquerading as Italian food?**

A: Impasta!

Q: **What has four fingers and a thumb but isn't living?**

A: A glove.

Q: **What can be swallowed but can also swallow you?**

A: Pride.

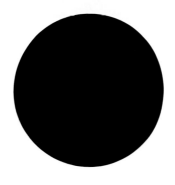

Q: What's made of wood but can't be sawed?

A: Saw dust.

Q: What side of the cat has the most fur?

A: The outside.

Does a hungry clock go back for seconds?

Q: What has ten letters and starts with gas?

A: An automobile.

Q: How many apples grow on trees?

A: All apples grow on trees.

Q: Why can't a T-Rex clap?

A: Because they are extinct.

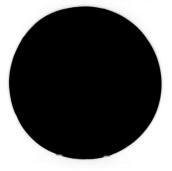

Q: **How do you make seven**
    even?

A: Take away the S.

Instead of being sad he was delighted when the
batteries in his flashlight went out.

Q: **What has a foot but no leg?**

A: A ruler.

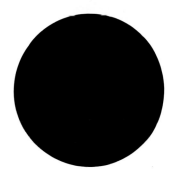

Her fear of moving stairs is escalating.

Q: What is the coolest letter of the alphabet?

A: B. It's always surrounded by AC.

Eggs are terrible comedians. They always crack up at their own jokes.

Q: What animal likes to learn?

A: Fish, they travel in schools!

Q: What would you call a fish with a missing eye?

A: A fish.

Q: What do you call a fancy fish?

A: Sofishticated.

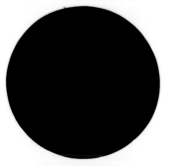

Q: Why was the broom late?

A: It overswept.

Without geometry, life is pointless.

Q: Why do bicycles fall over?

A: Because they're two-tired.

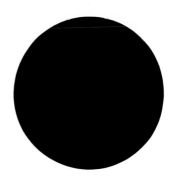

Q: **Why is the calendar so popular?**

A: Because it has so many dates.

Math teachers have a lot of problems.

Q: **Why do you go to bed every night?**

A: Because the bed won't come to you.

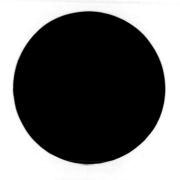

Q: **What do lawyers wear to court?**

A: Lawsuits.

Q: **Why did the little pigs fall asleep when grandpa told a story?**

A: Because Grandpa was a boar.

Q: **What do you get when you cross an apple with a Christmas tree?**

A: A pineapple.

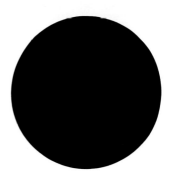

**Q: How do you make the
number one disappear?**

A: Add a G to it and it's gone.

Bananas are one of the most appealing fruits.

People who believe in ghosts are very ghoulable.

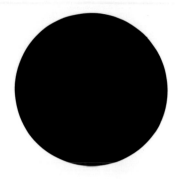

**Q: What do Pandas have that
no other animal has?**

A: Baby pandas.

Q: What did 0 say to 8?

A: "Nice belt."

**Q: What happened to the guy who had his whole
left side removed?**

A: He was all right.

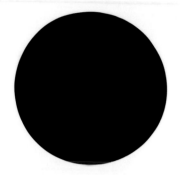

Q: **How do celebrities stay cool?**

A: They have a lot of fans.

Q: **Who walks into a restaurant, wastes shoots and leaves?**

A: A panda

Q: **Which hand is better to write with?**

A: Neither. It's better to use a pen or a pencil.

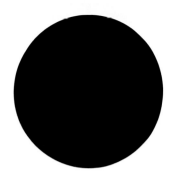

Q: **What can even the most careful person overlook?**

A: Their nose.

Q: **What is the capital of Alaska?**

A: A.

A boiled egg for breakfast is hard to beat.

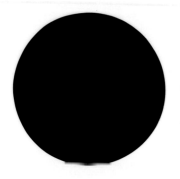

Q: What did Delaware?

A: Her New Jersey.

Q: Why is England the wettest country?

A: Because the queen has reigned there for years.

Q: Where was the Declaration of Independence signed?

A: On the bottom.

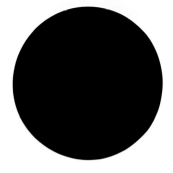

Simple as 3.14

Q: How can sea captains use
amphibians?

A: As froghorns.

Some river valleys are absolutely gorges.

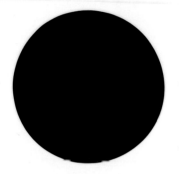

Q: **How many sides does a circle have?**

A: Two. Inside and outside.

She stayed up all night to see where the sun went and then it dawned on her.

He started working at a bakery because he kneaded dough.

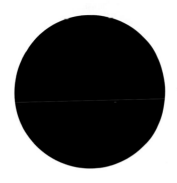

Q: How do you communicate with fish?

A: Drop them a line.

A backwards poet writes inverse.

Every calendar's days are numbered.

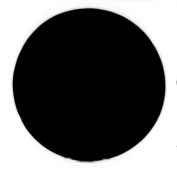

Q: **What musical is about a train conductor?**

A: "My Fare Lady"

Q: **Why do ambassadors never get sick?**

A: Diplomatic immunity.

Q: **Why did the robber shower before she robbed a bank?**

A: She wanted to make a clean getaway.

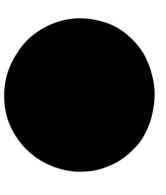

Q: Why did the man run around his bed?

A: He was trying to catch up on sleep.

Q: Why don't traffic lights go swimming?

A: Because they take too long to change.

Q: What does even the most careful person overlook?

A: Their nose.

Q: **Why was the belt arrested?**

A: Because it held up a pair of pants.

Q: **What's the difference between a TV and a newspaper?**

A: Have you ever tried to swat a fly with a TV?

Q: **What did the paper say to the pencil?**

A: Write on!

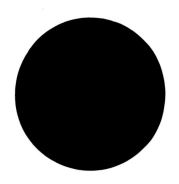

Q: Why can't you tell an egg a joke?

A: Because it might crack up.

Q: What can be full but never overflow?

A: The moon.

Q: What can you keep after giving it to someone else?

A: Your word.

Q: What goes around the wood but never goes into the wood?

A: The rings of a tree.

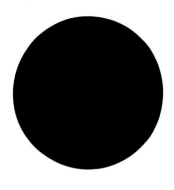

Q: **Where's the best place to look for a key?**

A: In a piano. It has tons of keys!

He tried to look for his missing clock but couldn't find the time.

Q: **What walks all day on its head?**

A: A nail in a horseshoe.

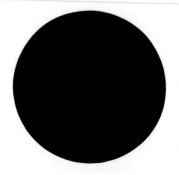

Q: **What has 13 hearts but no other organs?**

A: A deck of playing cards.

She used to hate math until she realized decimals had a point.

Q: **What dies but can be brought back to life with a simple charge?**

A: A battery.

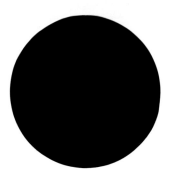

Q: What lives without a body, hears without ears, and speaks without a mouth?

A: An echo.

Q: Who always has a date?

A: A Calendar.

Q: What part of the snake is musical?

A: The scales.

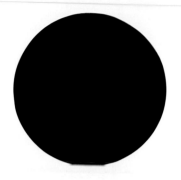

Q: **What can you never eat for dinner?**

A: Breakfast or lunch.

Q: **What is the beginning of eternity and the end of time and space?**

A: The letter E.

Q: **Why does lightning shock people?**

A: Because it doesn't know how to conduct itself.

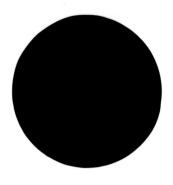

Q: What's the most musical animal you'll find in water?

A: Fish—they have scales!

Q: What falls but never hits the ground?

A: The temperature.

Q: What kind of awards do dentists get?

A: Plaques.

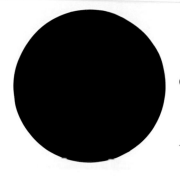

Q: **What does a dentist do during an earthquake?**

A: She braces herself.

Q: **Why did the tree go to the dentist?**

A: To get a root canal.

Q: **What stands on one leg with its heart on its head?**

A: Cabbage.

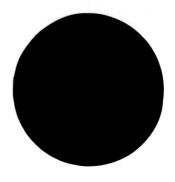

Q: What is full of holes but holds water?

A: A sponge.

Q: What goes up the stairs even though it doesn't move?

A: A rug.

Puns about ants bug me.

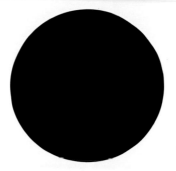

**She had a photographic
memory but never developed
it.**

Q: When prices go up, what remains stationary?

A: Writing paper and envelopes.

Q: What kind of can doesn't need a can opener?

A: A pelican.

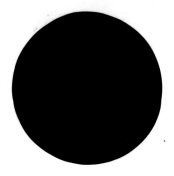

Q: What is the best month for a parade?

A: March!

Q: Why was the picture sent to jail?

A: Because it was framed.

Q: Where was the pencil store located?

A: Pennsylvania

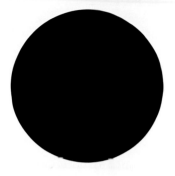

Q: What do you get when you pour cement on a thief?

A: A hardened criminal.

Closing the window to keep the bugs out is such a pane.

Q: What five-letter word sounds the same if you take away the first and last letter?

A: Empty.

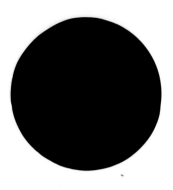

Q: What word is smaller when you add two letters to it?

A: Small.

You can usually bank on a river full of fish.

Q: What road vehicle has four wheels and flies?

A: A garbage truck.

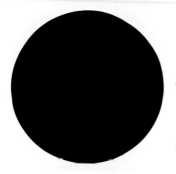

11

Q: What has four legs, a head, and a foot?

A: A bed.

Q: Where does a trout deposit his money?

A: A riverbank.

Q: Why do ghosts like to haunt libraries?

A: They like being around the BOOks.

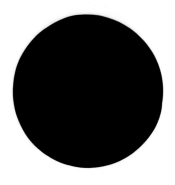

Q: Can February March?

A: No, but April May.

Everyone was so tired on April 1st. They had just finished a March of 31 days.

Q: What is it that after you take away the whole some still remains?

A: Wholesome.

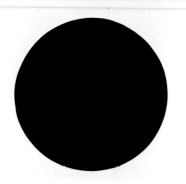

Looking for more laughs?

Check out the other two books in the Belly Laugh series!

Are you a Minecraft fan in need of a good laugh?

Check out our Minecraft joke books!

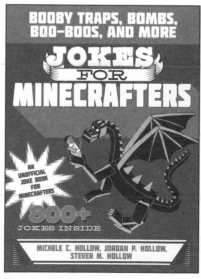